GOD'S GENERALS

FOR KIDS

JOHN G. LAKE

GOD'S GENERALS

FOR KIDS

JOHN G. LAKE

BY
ROBERTS LIARDON
& OLLY GOLDENBERG

BRIDGE
LOGOS

Newberry, FL 32669

Bridge-Logos
Newberry, Florida 32669 USA

God's Generals For Kids — John G. Lake
Roberts Liardon & Olly Goldenberg

Copyright ©2015 Roberts Liardon & Olly Goldenberg
Reprint 2020

Printed in the United States of America.

Library of Congress Catalog Card Number: 2015930174

International Standard Book Number 978-1-61036-207-8

Unless otherwise noted, all Scripture is from the King James Version of the Bible.

The photographs used are owned by and taken from the private collection of Roberts Liardon.

Timeline illustrations by David Parfitt.

JOHN G. LAKE

CONTENTS

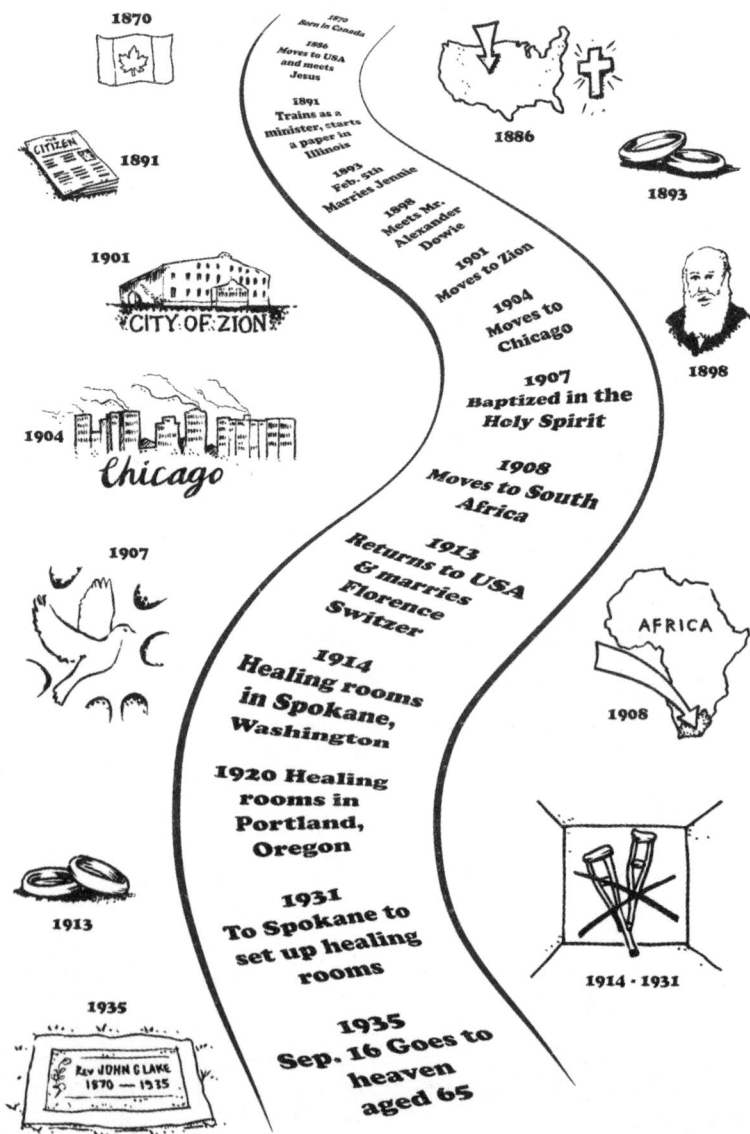

TIMELINE

1870

1891

1901
CITY OF ZION

1904
Chicago

1907

1913

1935
Rev JOHN G LAKE
1870 — 1935

1870
Born in Canada

1886
Moves to USA
and meets
Jesus

1891
Trains as a
minister, starts
a paper in
Illinois

1893
Feb. 5th
Marries Jennie

1898
Meets Mr.
Alexander
Dowie

1901
Moves to Zion

1904
Moves to
Chicago

1907
Baptized in the
Holy Spirit

1908
Moves to South
Africa

1913
Returns to USA
& marries
Florence
Switzer

1914
Healing rooms
in Spokane,
Washington

1920 Healing
rooms in
Portland,
Oregon

1931
To Spokane to
set up healing
rooms

1935
Sep. 16 Goes to
heaven
aged 65

1886

1893

1898

1908
AFRICA

1914 · 1931

CHAPTER 1

A LIFE OF SICKNESS

John, upper left, with surviving Lake family members. 8 of his original brothers and sisters died from disease.

ONE BIG FAMILY

How would you feel if you grew up in a family with fifteen other children? It would be pretty busy, you would probably share your room with several other people and you wouldn't have any personal space.

You would all be squashed into a house unless you had a 17 bedroom mansion. Your family would have to get along well with each other because you lived so close together. You would have to love your brothers and sisters (even if you didn't really like them). Whatever you thought about them, they'd be a key part of your life.

But what if half of them died?

That was what happened to John Lake. When he was growing up his family was big and he was surrounded by death. It seemed like sickness was in charge of his home. His parents were healthy but everybody else suffered at one time or another.

When a family member became sick John would be there watching it all take place. He'd seen it happen so often to someone in his family. He knew the routine. First the doctors and nurses would be called in to look after them. Then there would be endless trips to and from the hospital to visit the latest sick brother or sister battling for their life. This would continue for some time until eventually the illness would win and the sibling would die.

Even as a child, John Lake knew what happened next. He had experienced it so many times in his young life. There would be a hearse to carry the coffin in to the funeral; then everyone would go to the graveyard. At the graveyard, the tombstone would be ready to be engraved with a few words on it that tried to sum up the life of yet another young member of his family.

The next few months would be sad and difficult. Mom and dad would be less interested in life as they faced grief again at the loss of another of their beloved children. They forced themselves to keep going because of the other children, but they wanted to give up. As everything started to get back to normal, someone else would fall sick.

Life definitely wasn't easy for John.

INSPIRED BY EXPLORERS

Other than all the death and sickness, John was a typical boy. He loved to play, he had friends. He did the same kind of things children all over the world do. John also loved to read; in fact he was pretty clever.

Some of his favorite books told the true stories of explorers who had lived before him. Just as you are reading about John Lake now who lived before you were born, John Lake did the same when he was your age and read about a man called David Livingstone. Another of his favorite books was about an explorer called Henry Stanley.

Now both of these men explored Africa. Although John was born in Canada back in 1870, as a child he always dreamed of going exploring in Africa, especially South Africa where David Livingstone had worked for a long time as a missionary. Sometimes the dreams were so real, that John would wake up in his bed thinking he was actually in Africa, not Canada.

Of course in those days it wasn't that easy to get from one country to another, you couldn't just hop on a plane, because they hadn't been invented yet. Instead you would have to go by boat. The boats would take three or four weeks to get there, so you wouldn't go for a week's vacation because if it took a month to get there, you knew it would take a month to get back again, so you knew you would be staying there for a little while.

With all the sickness in his family and because he was only a child it didn't look like his dream was going to happen soon. But children don't stay as children for long—they grow up. Sometimes the things we dream of as children are the very things that God is calling us to when we grow up. John Lake was going to find this out many years later.

THE GOOD GOSPEL

When he was still young John moved with his family, from Canada, to Michigan in America. At the age of around sixteen he heard something he'd never heard before. He heard the Gospel of Jesus being preached in a meeting run by the Salvation Army.

John was a good man. He hadn't done anything majorly wrong in his life and he'd certainly never be in trouble with the police. But from the day he heard the Gospel something bothered him. He heard how Jesus came to help sinners, and deep down he knew that he had sinned. The preacher explained that everyone is a sinner until they ask Jesus into their heart. He knew he hadn't broken any laws in America or in Canada, but now he knew and understood how he had failed God.

No matter what he did John could not run away from his sin and this really bothered him. The more he thought about it, the more he thought about what the preacher had said in the meeting. The more he thought about what the preacher said, the more he thought about his sin. God was working in him.

The preacher had told John that Jesus Christ is God's Son and that He has the power to forgive us and take away our sins and John knew this was what he needed. He knelt down and prayed, "Jesus, please forgive me and take my sins away. I want to follow you for the rest of my life. I am sorry for the things I have done wrong. I choose to put you in charge of my life from now on. I want everything to be alright between me and God so I can be one of His sons, and He can do whatever He wants with me for the rest of my life."

When John stood up he knew that God had forgiven him of all his sins and that he was now one of God's sons. All the sin and guilt that had been bothering him were gone forever. Now he just wanted to serve God.

God had great plans for John, but first John had to learn a bit more about God.

A MAN OF SCIENCE

John loved learning. He especially loved learning about science and he loved to do science experiments. In fact he loved it so much that he decided to put his love of science to good use. As a child he had seen so many doctors helping his family that he decided to study medicine for himself. This gave him loads of opportunities to examine people who were sick.

John was curious. He loved examining things and he always wanted to test what people said to find out what was actually true. If someone had told him that you can stay under water for twenty minutes, John would have wanted to jump into the nearest pool and time how long he could stay under water. If someone said that salt could make a sick person better, John would have wanted to grab some salt and find the nearest sick person to try it out.

Neither of these things work by the way, unless of course you are only holding a cup of water over your head and standing under it, instead of sticking your head into the water. Actually you could stick your head underwater for twenty minutes but you would need a snorkel or something else to help you breathe so that doesn't really count either. Salt doesn't make sick people better unless they don't have enough of it in their body. In general salt isn't very good for you and most people have far too much of it already. So now you don't need to try out either of these things.

Anyway, John knew that reading the Bible was a really important way to get to know God. As a scientist, he didn't just want to read the nice stories in the Bible, he wanted to examine the Bible and do the things it said to do in his own life. If the Bible said when you pray for someone they will get better, John wasn't happy reading about it. He wanted to experience it for himself. John wanted to live out every bit of the Bible.

By the time John was twenty a farmer showed him from the Bible how he could be made holy by God and live a life set apart for God, simply by doing what the Bible said. Well this was pretty life-changing for John.

He didn't finish his studies in medicine, but a year after he learned about holiness he moved to Chicago and went to a Methodist Bible school to prepare to be a minister. After lots of training, they asked him to be the minister in a church. John said, "No". Instead he went to Harvey, Illinois to run a newspaper. In the days before television, everybody read newspapers and just about every town had a local newspaper.

John called the newspaper he published "The Harvey Citizen." It wasn't a national newspaper, as you may have guessed from the title—but it was very popular and was read by many of the citizens who lived in Harvey. John was good at the publishing business and he did really well. In fact he could have stayed there for years.

But God had other plans for John.

CHAPTER 2

GETS A BEATING

John G. Lake

MEETING JOHN DOWIE

John grew up surrounded by sickness. However, being surrounded by it and being sick yourself are two completely different things. While John was still young his legs started to ache a bit. He went to several doctors who told him that he had rheumatism and they couldn't make it better. His legs started to ache more and more until the ache became constant pain. Not only that, but his legs started to look misshapen and deformed. It was like his body wasn't his own any more. He felt like he was being kicked out of it and the disease was taking over.

John was in so much pain. He couldn't take it. "The doctors can't help me, I wonder if God can?" John thought to himself. The only person he had seen healed was a lady in his Methodist church. He'd also heard about a man called John Alexander Dowie who had prayed and seen lots of people healed. (You can read about the life of John Alexander Dowie in volume 3 of the God's Generals for Kids series).

Now, Mr. Dowie ran a special healing home in Chicago. So John went to Chicago to see if God would heal him. When he got there his legs were so painful he could barely move them enough to drag himself into the healing room and sit down.

An older man came and put his hands on John and started to pray. As soon as he prayed John felt the presence of God, his legs straightened out, and the pain disappeared completely. The disease that had been trying to kick him out of his own body was now kicked out by God. John was free at last.

For the first time, John discovered for himself that there was something more powerful than sickness. Sickness and disease had been battering his family far too long. Now John knew that God could beat it.

HEAL MY FAMILY TOO

He rushed home and grabbed his brother. His brother had been sick for many years, and it looked like he wasn't going to be alive much longer.

"You have to come with me," John said. "I've been healed by God and God can heal you too."

His brother was hardly able to stand because he was so sick, so John carried him to Mr. Dowie's home. People came and put their hands on his brother and prayed for him as he lay in a bed, half dead. Immediately he leapt out of the bed and was completely healed. He'd been sick for twenty-two years and in less than twenty-two minutes God completely healed him.

The next one needing healing in John's family was his sister, who had breast cancer. There was no cure for breast cancer in those days. The only thing left for the doctors to do was to try to make her comfortable, until she died. Even though the doctors were giving her lots of medicine, she did not feel very comfortable. She was so weak that she had to be carried everywhere. She also had a lot of pain. In spite of all the medicines she could still feel the pain, day and night. It was very painful for John to see his sister suffering so much.

John now knew that God healed people and he was not going to stand by and watch his sister die. John had decided: "God I am going to bring my sister to you. I know you can heal and I believe you are going to heal my sister."

Even though the cancer was spreading from one big lump into smaller lumps, even though his sister didn't believe that God could heal her, even though she was preparing to die, and even though the rest of the family and the doctors had all given up hope, John knew that God could heal her.

He took her to Mr. Dowie's healing home. She stayed there for several days and people prayed for her. While she was there, she listened to people preaching from the Bible. After a little while she started to believe what it said in the Bible. She believed that God could heal her.

Immediately the pain disappeared and she felt so much better. A few days later a big lump fell off her body, it was the cancer. It wasn't supposed to be on her body, so God cut it off! The smaller lumps were still on her, but the main lump of the cancer had been completely cut off and you could hold it in your hands!

A few days later the smaller lumps disappeared. There was not one spot of disease left in her. God had completely healed her.

So God had healed John, his brother and his sister at Mr. Dowie's healing rooms. Can you imagine how excited John felt? For his whole life he had seen people he loved die. Now God was healing the people he loved.

CAN GOD CONQUER DEATH?

John couldn't stop yet. There were more people in his family who were sick. John planned to take another of his sisters who was also dying. As with the other siblings, the doctors had given up all hope. This didn't stop John. He now knew that God was far more powerful than any doctor.

As he was getting ready to take his sister to Mr. Dowie's home, he got a phone call from his Mother. "John, your sister is dying. If you want to see her before she dies, you need to come quickly." John rushed to the house.

When he got there, the room was full of people. They were all crying. His sister was lying on her bed and she wasn't moving. Everyone in the room knew what had happened. Trembling, John tried to find her pulse. It was not there. She was dead.

John was devastated. He remembered all the people he loved who had died. Now there was one more. He wasn't the only person who was suffering. Beside his sister's bed there was a cot and in the cot was his sister's baby. John looked at the baby. Lying there by itself, it was so small and alone. "This baby *can't* grow up without it's mom," he thought. "My sister has to live, she has to be with her baby and look after it."

John knew that God could heal people who were sick. He also knew that in the Bible, Jesus had raised some people from the dead. He walked up and down the room as he thought about it. John needed somebody else who would pray with him, someone else who really believed that God could make his sister live again.

He looked around the room, everyone was crying. None of them would be able to help him. In fact, John could only think of one man who really believed God could do such an impossible thing, Mr. Dowie.

So John sent a message to Mr. Dowie, "My sister has apparently died, but my spirit will not let her go. I believe that if you pray, God will heal her."

John had to wait a little while, before Mr. Dowie replied, "Hold on to God. I am praying. She will live."

As John read the message his faith in God exploded. He knew God could heal his sister, and John was going to keep on praying until she was alive again. It was like he was fighting with death as he prayed over her. He told death to leave his sister alone in the name of Jesus. God's power is so great, and John's faith was so strong, that death had to obey. After an hour of prayer his sister sat up. She was alive! A few days later, it was Christmas day. She was back to normal and joined the rest of the family for Christmas dinner.

CHAPTER 3

HIS WIFE'S SICKNESS

John and his first wife: Jennie

SICKNESS FOLLOWS THE FAMILY

John's life was getting better and better. His newspaper business was doing really well and he was learning more about God. He also was starting his own family.

John had met a lovely lady called Jennie Stevens. She was a lady who loved God and knew how to pray. When they got married on February 5th, 1893, it was a really happy day.

Their home was filled with fun, lots of laughter, lots of happiness and eventually there were going to be lots of children too—seven in all. John and Jennie often prayed together and when they were not together, they prayed for each other. Everything was very different from John's family. It all seemed perfect ... until two years into their marriage something awful happened. No one could have predicted it. For John it was the most devastating thing that could have happened.

His wife became sick.

Jennie had a disease called tuberculosis (or TB for short). She coughed, she lost weight, and she became weak. It affected everything she did. She found it hard to cook a meal for the family and hard to sleep at night, because she was so sick.

Not only that, but Jennie's heart wasn't working properly. Instead of beating regularly, it would beat randomly. Sometimes it couldn't even pump hard enough to get her blood to flow through her body. When that happened she would collapse onto the floor, unconscious.

Imagine that! She could be in the middle of chatting to a friend or cleaning the house, then suddenly she would collapse without warning.

Sometimes John would walk into a room and find her lying on the floor, not able to move and not aware of anything going on around her, completely unconscious. At other times she would go to bed, too sick to do anything.

If you met her, even on a good day, you would have known immediately that she was sick. Her voice was weak, she moved slowly and she looked sick.

John just couldn't get away from sickness.

Of course the doctors did their best to make Jennie better. They gave her all kinds of medicine, but nothing seemed to help. In the end the medicine they gave her was so strong that she could no longer live a normal life. Still she didn't get better.

This went on for years.

IS THERE ANY HOPE?

John had to do many things around the home, while still running his newspaper business. He was tired, but more than that he was facing a crisis. The doctors had tried everything they could think of. There was nothing else they could do for Jennie. John prayed for her, but she was still sick.

John was broken. Illness seemed to follow him, wherever he went. Every time he tried to get away from sickness, it was waiting around the corner wanting to catch up with him. John was fed up with it.

John spent much time praying for his wife. But she still did not get better. John felt utterly powerless, and though he'd seen God do some amazing healings, the more he prayed for Jennie the sicker she became.

One day a friend of his came around to visit. He was a minister and had helped many people cope when their relatives were dying. Now Jennie was dying. She had a temperature, she couldn't even get out of bed, she was the sickest she had ever been. The minister knew that the end was near. "John," he said, "she is going to die. This is obviously what God wants. You have to let her go."

But John couldn't do it. Even though it looked like she could die any minute, John had already seen too much death in his life. He was not prepared to accept her death. The minister seemed to think she had only a few hours left to live. John planned to spend the rest of his life with her.

He felt so hopeless. He knew the God of the Bible could heal her, but she was not healed. He'd seen God heal his brother and sisters and he'd even been healed himself, but Jennie was still sick.

What was wrong? How could God let this happen? He was so frustrated.

FINDING POWER IN GOD'S WORD

He picked up his Bible and threw it against the fireplace. As it fell to the floor the Bible opened up at Luke chapter 10. John walked over and picked up the Bible, his eyes were drawn to verse 38, "... God anointed Jesus of Nazareth with the Holy Spirit and with power: who went about doing good, and healing all that were oppressed of the devil, for God was with him."

As he read the verse, four words spun around in his head: 'OPPRESSED OF THE DEVIL.' They were the only words he could think about. Suddenly he realized that Jennie was not sick because God wanted her to die. John knew that Jennie was sick, because of the devil.

The devil was playing his usual tricks. The devil had made her sick and now the devil was trying to steal his wife. The devil was trying to kill his children's mother. In fact, John suddenly realized that the devil was trying to ruin his life, by taking Jennie from him! At last things made sense.

John quickly turned in the Bible to Luke chapter 13:16. There he read how Jesus healed a woman who had a bent back. People tried to stop Jesus from doing it, but Jesus said "shouldn't this woman, who Satan has bound for eighteen years, be set free." Jesus had completely healed the woman; surely Jesus could heal his wife too.

John knew that Jesus had set him free from sin. After all that was why Jesus died on the Cross. John knew that because of this he was now a child of God. So if the Son of God could set a woman free from the work of the devil, then he, as a child of God, could do the same things that Jesus did.

After all, if Jesus had taken away his sins, and his wife's sins, when He died on the Cross, then Jesus could easily take away this sickness. If God could heal the woman in Luke 13, then God could also heal his wife. Now John finally realized that Satan was the cause of her sickness, he also knew that the sickness had already been conquered by Jesus on the Cross.

TIME TO BE HEALED

All this time, while John was getting revelation from God, Jennie lay dying on her bed. God's power come on John and he marched up to her bedroom. When he went into the room he spoke out loud, "My wife is going to be healed at exactly 9.30 this morning."

He wanted everyone in the room to know what God was going to do. He also wanted the devil, and anyone else who may be listening in, to know what was about to happen.

It was less than a year since Mr. Dowie had prayed for John's siblings to be healed. Mr. Dowie had also been praying for Jennie's healing too. John called him, "God is going to heal Jennie at 9.30 in the morning." This wasn't John's idea, the Holy Spirit was making John bold!

When 9.30 came, John quietly knelt next to Jennie, and prayed for her once more. He simply asked God to heal her. Then God came and took over. John heard a quiet sound come from her mouth. He leaned in close to see if she was trying to whisper something.

But she didn't whisper anything. Instead she shouted, "Praise God, I'm healed!" right into his ear. John jumped backwards.

Jennie hadn't spoken like this for years. Jennie could move, she could breathe, she wasn't coughing, her heart was back to normal, and she had no temperature. John had his wife back.

She threw back the bed covers and stood up. John and Jennie praised God together. She'd been sick for three long years. Now, at 9.30 a.m., on April 28th 1898, she was completely, totally, permanently, healed by God.

Jennie's healing opened up a whole new chapter in John's life.

CHAPTER 4

GROWING IN THE HEALING MINISTRY

John Lake

THE SICK COME

People were amazed when they saw that Jennie was well. News of the healing traveled all over the country. Before long, sick people started to come to John's home, asking him to pray for them. Other people sent requests to him, asking him to pray for their healing.

God had started this ministry by healing John's family. John knew he really needed God's help. As John sat in a meeting he listened to the preacher speaking, "you need to be baptized in the Holy Spirit. God gives you His power when you are baptized in His spirit."

John knelt down "God, baptize me with your Holy Spirit." As he prayed, John felt God's presence come upon him and he suddenly became aware of God's power in a totally new way. Just like the sea waves wash onto the beach, John felt the waves of God's power washing onto him.

John started to get really busy. He ran his business and looked after his family, and now lots of sick people came to him to ask for prayers as well.

One day John went to visit a man who had a high temperature and a sore on his skin that was the size of a dinner plate! John put his hand on the sore and prayed for God to take it away. Before long John received a message from the man: "an hour after you left me I could see the print of your hand burned into the growth. Your hand print was about half a centimeter deep!"

I NEED TO LEARN MORE

John realized that God had given him a gift of healing, now he wanted to learn more about it. He left his newspaper business and moved to a city that Mr. Dowie had built, called Zion.

Mr. Dowie asked John to look after all of his buildings. In the daytime John looked after buildings. In the evenings John was out preaching to people. His studies on healing had to be fitted in around everything else.

One day John went to a meeting in his friend's house. That night there was a man preaching, called Tom Hezmalhalch. Tom was older than John, he had a moustache and his hair was greying. As he taught John noticed an authority in his preaching. The Holy Spirit was clearly in Tom's life.

At the end of the meeting, Tom came up to John. He told him bluntly, "As I was preaching, Jesus told me that you and I are going to preach together."

John found it funny at first. They had only just met; Tom was far more experienced in the ministry. A few days later God spoke to John directly and John realized that Tom was right. This was what God wanted them to do.

Tom and John became best of friends, working together and preaching together many times.

MOVING AWAY

John carried on his work in Zion, until he became concerned about some of the things Mr. Dowie was doing. It seemed that Mr. Dowie had problems with money. More serious still, John also thought that Mr. Dowie was starting to move away from the teaching in the Bible. It was time for him to leave the city of Zion.

In 1904 John moved, with his family, to Chicago. When he got there, John paid to be a part of the Chicago board of trade. This was a large organization where all the top businessmen did business with each other. John got to know people and was soon making lots of money.

Within a year he had become extremely rich. He was so good at making money that some businessmen asked John to run three of the biggest insurance companies of the nation. John was one of the top businessmen in Chicago. People would come to him and pay him to give them advice. It seemed that no matter what he did, money came pouring into his pocket.

But John was not trying to make money; John wanted to serve God more. During all this time John also continued to grow with God. God continued to work in John to prepare him for his call.

CHAPTER 5

GOD STIRRING INSIDE HIM

John Lake with friends

HUNGRY FOR GOD

John still wanted more. Even with all of the amazing miracles he was seeing God do, he wanted more of God. God was using John to do great miracles, more than many other ministers around him. Yet John was still not satisfied.

29

What John really wanted was the Baptism of the Holy Spirit.

Many years ago John was prayed for, and at that time he had experienced God's presence. Since then, God had used John. John saw many prayers answered and some people were healed. Yet John was still asking God to baptize him in the Holy Spirit.

John's friends were confused. "John, what do you mean you want to be baptized in the Spirit? You already are! If you weren't you wouldn't be seeing all the miracles that you see when you pray." John didn't agree. He still wanted so much more of God. He felt he had not had everything that God had planned.

WHAT IS BAPTISM?

The word 'baptism' means to be fully covered. So baptism in the Holy Spirit would mean to be fully covered in the Spirit of God. John expected that he would be ministering at a completely different level if that happened to him. He would be doing the same kind of things that Jesus did, in the same way, at the same level.

When you go to the seaside you can dip your toe in the sea and you get a bit of a feeling of what it is like, but it is not the same as swimming in the sea, completely surrounded by the water. John felt he had dipped his toe into the Holy Spirit, now he wanted to be completely covered by the Holy Spirit. John knew that he had only begun to meet God.

This desire for God grew so much that John had to do something. He set aside several hours a day, to think about God and to pray. After many months of waiting for God each day, the Holy Spirit spoke to him: "John, you need to wait until the autumn."

He was so happy. He carried on praying and thinking about God. In fact it became such a habit that he was able to focus on God when he was doing something completely different. Wherever John went he was always talking quietly to God.

As well as spending hours each day with God, John continued to work in the day. Most nights he was out preaching, and after the meetings he often met with friends to ask God to baptize them in the Holy Spirit, so that they would be completely filled by Him.

You may wonder how he managed to spend so much time praying when he was doing all these other things—he did it because he was hungry for more of God. If you've ever been really hungry for food, you'll know that it takes over your thoughts. You may be trying to do your school work, but when you are hungry it is hard to concentrate. All you can think about is what you are going to eat and when you are going to get to eat it. Your hunger is there, interrupting everything you are doing, until, at the very least, you can find something to snack on to keep you going.

John was hungry for God. Thoughts of seeking God invaded everything else that he did. Yes he'd seen God doing great things through him, but he wanted more of God: so much that this thought filled every second of his day.

BAPTIZED IN THE HOLY SPIRIT

When autumn came a woman visited his church. She saw how much John wanted God, so she put her hands on his head and prayed that he would be baptized in the Holy Spirit. Nothing seemed to happen at that time.

That afternoon his friend, Tom, asked John to go with him to minister to a lady who was crippled because of aching joints and arthritis. She had been suffering for ten years, and now the only way she could get around was by using a wheel chair.

As soon as they arrived, Tom chatted away with her. He wanted her to know that God could heal her, so that she would be ready when they prayed. Meanwhile John sat in a chair on the other side of the room. As he sat there, every cell in his body was crying out for God.

Suddenly he felt like a shower of warm rain was falling onto him. He felt so calm and for the first time in his life he felt a deep peace. He knew that God was responding to his hunger.

God spoke to him: "John, I've heard your prayers, I've seen you crying because you want me so much. You are now baptized in the Holy Spirit."

GOD'S ELECTRICITY

The feeling of rain stopped, but the feeling of peace stayed. It was so beautiful. John then began to feel currents of power going through him. It was like electricity. The power was so great that John started to shake, he could not sit still. God was all over him. John was finally filled with the Holy Spirit.

The lightning bolts of God's power moved all over his body, from his feet up to his mouth. As soon as it reached his mouth strange words started to come out. He couldn't speak in English, instead he found himself speaking a language that he had never been taught. John was speaking in tongues!

Remember, John was a scientist. He wanted proof of everything. Sure, he was having a wonderful experience, but he needed to know if it was really God and not his imagination. God was about to show him.

Tom had nearly finished talking with the lady and was getting ready to pray. He'd been so busy talking that he hadn't noticed what was going on with John. He asked John to come and join him to pray for the lady to be healed.

As John got up he was trembling all over. He could hardly walk because his legs were shaking from the experience he'd had. Not only that, his arms were shaking too. "We are praying for pain to leave her joints," John thought. "If I touch her while I'm shaking like this I will end up shaking her and causing her more pain. I'll just touch her gently with the tips of my fingers."

As he touched her head with his fingertips he felt God's power passing through him to the lady. The lady felt it too.

Tom hadn't noticed anything, but now he was ready to pray. He gently took hold of the lady's hand and immediately felt God's power flowing through her. It was so strong that Tom fell onto the floor. He looked up and saw John touching her head and knew that God's power had flowed through John, into the lady and on into him. "Praise the Lord, John," Tom cried out, "Jesus has baptized you in the Holy Ghost."

Then Tom looked at the lady's hands. They had been clenched shut for years, warped by the disease. As he watched the fingers started to move, then the wrists could move, then the elbow and up to the shoulder. Bit by bit she was able to move every joint in her body. God had completely healed her.

John was rejoicing about something else. God had finally baptized him with the Holy Spirit. God had answered his prayer. With the baptism he had God's power, but more than that he experienced God's love for people. Not only could John feel God's love, but he felt Jesus' character inside him. No longer was he full of himself, now he was full of Jesus' Spirit.

CHAPTER 6

LIVING ONLY FOR GOD

John Lake and campaign workers

GOD AT WORK INSIDE

After he was baptized in the Holy Spirit, John expected to see lots more miracles when he prayed. But he didn't. Instead the Holy Spirit started to point out things in his life that he had to change. It took six months for God to show John everything he needed to see.

John had to repent a lot and to make many changes in his life. Once he had made the changes he found that he loved people much more. After this love, came God's power. Whenever John preached now, miracles and healings took place.

John's new infilling in the Holy Spirit caused him to have a problem. Now he could only see things from God's perspective. This was no problem when he was ministering in the church, but when he was at work he could not focus properly on what he was supposed to be doing. Everywhere he looked he saw how much people needed God.

WORTH MORE THAN MONEY

One day at work John had a very important meeting with a man. If the meeting went well he would earn thousands of dollars. When the man walked in, John could not focus on the meeting, because something else was bothering him.

As he looked at the man, it was as if God was letting him see right into the man's soul. He saw that he was a man who did not know God, and he also saw that God really loved him. The man was like a lost sheep needing to be led back to God. It was as if the man was walking around, not really knowing what his purpose was in life, looking for something more.

John felt like his heart was going to explode: he was so sad to see how badly this man needed God. Instead of doing the business they had planned to do, John asked the man to kneel on the floor next to him. There at his work place, in his office, John knelt and prayed for the man, crying out for his salvation. By the end of the meeting the man had given his life to Christ.

This started to happen more and more as God opened his eyes to the state of people's souls. John was burdened for the lost with a love he had never experienced before.

TIME TO GO

In the end John had to speak to his boss. He knew he couldn't do the job he was being paid to do properly. More importantly, God's call on his life was now so strong that he had to fulfil it.

"I can't do this anymore," John said to his boss. "I am so concerned to see people come to know God that I can't do what you are paying me to do."

His boss looked at him, "John, you have worked so hard. Why don't you go on holiday for three months? If you feel you want to preach, then spend time preaching. But after those three months your salary will seem like a lot of money.

You won't want to give up all that money to go and do your religious things."

John left, knowing that he had done the right thing. He never looked back.

During those three months John preached every day to large numbers of people. People were saved, people were healed and hundreds of people were baptized in the Holy Spirit. By the end of the three months John spoke his heart to God, "I am not going to do anything else in this life, except preach about Jesus and show people He exists by the miracles He does."

John was very wealthy. By today's standards he would be a millionaire. He was so successful in business. He had everything you could ever want. But he had decided to give up everything that he had to preach the Gospel. John took all of his possessions, his home and every other thing he owned and sold it.

Then he gave away every single cent.

John had decided to depend completely on God to provide for his needs and the needs of his family. He was going to focus on preaching about Jesus.

SCIENTIFIC PROOF

John prayed for so many people and saw some amazing things happen around this time. John knew that God was healing people, now he wanted scientific proof of God's power at work. He went to a clinic to do some experiments, hoping to find out how God worked through his body when he was ministering.

In one experiment, they put some wires on his head, to measure his brain activity. Then John began to think about God. As he thought about God, the needle on the display showed that there was a lot of activity in his brain. Then John started to pray and as he prayed the Holy Spirit came upon him. At that moment the activity in John's brain became so great that the needle went right up to maximum and could go no further.

The scientists were puzzled by this. John explained to them that God was filling his brain. As God is so great, He could not be measured.

John loved to prove to the scientists that God really was God. Having learned a bit about being a doctor, John wanted the doctors to see that God was more powerful than them.

Sometimes people would come to him, because the doctors did not know what to do. At this time, God gave John a special gift. By touching the sick person, John could tell what part of the body was not working properly, how bad it was and the exact place where the problem was.

John would go to the hospitals, when the doctors did not know what to do, and use this gift to see people healed. He loved playing with the new gift.

Until one day he couldn't do it anymore—the gift stopped working.

GOD OR THE GIFT?

John talked to God about it. He realized that he had made a big mistake: he wanted to use the gift, more than he wanted to meet with God. He said, "Sometimes, a child can play with a toy and enjoy playing with it so much that he forgets to eat."

John realized he had been so busy using and playing with the gift that he had forgotten to take the spiritual food that God gives us in the Bible and through prayer. When we walk close to God, God will give us supernatural gifts to use. These gifts should never be the focus of our lives. God himself must be the focus.

John had to repent and put God first again. He had learned a valuable lesson that would help him in the future. John was ready to see what God wanted him to do.

GET READY TO MOVE

One night John was praying. The Holy Spirit showed him a number of different cities. "John, I am going to send you for five years to each of these places that I am showing you." The Holy Spirit showed him exactly what was going to happen there. The last place the Holy Spirit showed him was a church in South Africa.

The vision John had was so clear. In the visions he saw his friend Tom with him. He also saw the entrance to the church building, what it looked like on the inside, and even the furniture that would be in the church.

A few months later, John was preaching in a city in Northern Illinois. As he was resting in his hotel he saw a boy who worked at the hotel. The boy was not very strong and he had to chop down a large tree, so he asked if anyone could help him. John volunteered, he loved to help people in any way that he could, because he loved people.

He was busy sawing the tree when he heard the Holy Spirit speak to him very clearly: "Go to Indianapolis. Prepare for a winter campaign. Get a large hall. In the spring you will go to Africa."

John finished chopping down the tree and went back to the hotel. Jennie, his dear wife, was there waiting for him.

John sat down and told her what God had said to him. He expected her to ask some questions, or even to want some time to pray about it.

Jennie smiled at him, "I know already," she said. "God told me a few days ago as I was praying that we had finished our work here and would be moving." She had been waiting for John to tell her where they were going to next.

John, Jennie and their children obeyed God together as they moved to Indianapolis, where God planned to do His final bit of preparation before sending John to Africa.

CHAPTER 7

TIME TO CAST OUT DEMONS

John Lake at a crusade

NO FOOD FOR ME

John and his family arrived in Indianapolis with great excitement. After only a few days of being there God had helped them to organize everything for the campaign. They had hired a large hall to hold the meetings in, just as God had told them to. Now they were busy getting everything else ready.

One morning John came down to breakfast. When he got downstairs he didn't really feel like eating, so he skipped breakfast and got on with his work. For the rest of the day he ate nothing. The next day he got up expecting to feel hungry, but he still did not want to eat.

By the end of the third day without food, John only wanted to pray. He did not know what he was praying for, he just needed to pray. For days he could not eat, and he did not even want to sleep. He kept praying and praying. John prayed whatever he was doing. When he was travelling along he prayed, as he worked he prayed. More than anything else he wanted to be alone, to kneel before God and pray.

After six days without food he was washing his hands, when God urged him to go and pray again. He knelt next to his bed and started praying. The Holy Spirit then spoke to him: "How long have you been praying for the power to cast out demons?"

John replied, "I've been praying for a long time, Lord."

God spoke: "From now on, you will cast out demons."

John got up and started to praise God. All of that time spent praying, had been to get him ready for this.

DO YOU ACTUALLY BELIEVE IT?

The next night, after John had finished preaching in the hall, a man came to speak to him. The man pointed to a sign on the wall where the words from the Bible in Mark 16:17 were written. It read, "In my name they shall cast out demons."

"Do you actually believe that verse is true?" the man asked.

John smiled, "I do."

"Are you sure," the man said, "because I have been looking for a minister who actually believes it. Many of them said they did, but they all went on to explain why it probably wouldn't happen."

John replied, "As sure as I know myself, I believe it with all my heart."

The man went on, "Let me tell you why I wanted to know. Two and a half years ago, my brother was in a church meeting. He had been asking God to make him holy, when suddenly he went completely crazy. The doctors came and locked him up in the mental hospital, because he was so crazy. The doctors say that it seems like his brain is completely normal, but he is still crazy. It seems that somehow he has been possessed by a demon. If you say that you believe that demons can be cast out in the name of God, I will take him out of the mental hospital this Sunday, bring him here and expect you to do it."

John was ready for this challenge, so he knelt with the man and prayed that the Holy Spirit would work on the people running the mental hospital so that they would allow him to come.

PROOF OF THE POWER

That Sunday John started the service, expecting God to do something great. The man had not arrived, but John was ready for him. John started to preach, and part way through his sermon, the man came in. His brother and a member of staff from the hospital were with him. John stopped preaching and called them forward.

As the man knelt at the front of the church, John asked some people to come forward and pray with him. He chose people who he knew loved God and were full of faith. While everyone was praying, John stepped off the platform, put his hands on the man's head and told the demon to come out of the man in the name of Jesus.

When John prayed he experienced the same feeling of electricity he had felt before. God's electricity shot through his body like a bolt of lightning and he knew at once that the man had been set free.

The man looked up and started to speak normally.

When he got back to the hospital, they told everyone there what had happened. The doctors examined him and asked him to stay for a few more days to make sure that he was actually better. On Wednesday they let him out of the hospital. By Thursday he was back at work.

God had not only told John that he had the power to cast out demons, now John had seen it with his own eyes. After all God knew that John didn't just want to learn about things, he wanted to see them in practice. John soon found out that God had not only given him His power, to cast out demons, but also God had also given him discernment: the ability to know when there was a demon in a person that needed to be cast out.

For the rest of the winter, John and Tom worked hard in Indianapolis, seeing many people saved, healed and now even delivered from demons. With this final gift from God, John was ready to begin what was to be the greatest chapter in his life.

CHAPTER 8

OFF TO AFRICA

John and Jennie Lake and their children before leaving for South Africa, 1907

PLEASE PROVIDE

By February 1908, John and Tom started to think about South Africa. God had said they would be going in spring. This meant they had a big hurdle to cross first: they had no money.

"How much will it cost, John, to take all of us to South Africa?" Tom asked.

John replied, "Two thousand dollars."

This was a huge amount of money; it would be the same as spending around fifty thousand dollars today.

Tom and John knew they would have to ask God for the money. After praying together for some time, Tom stood up and slapped John on the back. "Don't pray anymore, John. Jesus told me that He will send us that $2000 and that it will be here in four days."

Exactly four days later, Tom came back from the post office and threw $2000 onto the table. "Here is the answer to our prayers!" Tom shouted. "Jesus has sent it. We are going to Africa!"

The man who sent the money also sent a letter to them. It said, "While I was standing in the bank at Monrovia, in California, the Lord told me to send you this money. The money is yours for you to do whatever God has told you to do with it."

John took the money and bought the tickets for South Africa.

SETTING SAIL

So, as God had told John, they were ready to go to South Africa. In April of 1908, John, his wife, Jennie, and their seven children together with Tom's family and three other friends set off for South Africa.

Although John used to be a millionaire, he had given it all away. Now he only had $1.50. This was all the money he had to pay for anything that they needed while they were on their way to Africa. They all got on a train to get to the boat. As their train left the station, a young man ran next to the train and threw $2 into the train. The Lake family were now the owners of $3.50.

John knew they needed more money. One of his workers had decided to join them for the first part of the journey. She only had a ticket to get as far as Detroit. John knew he would have to pay for her to do the rest of the journey, even though it cost $10.

He spoke to Jennie, "We've got to pay for her ticket and we don't have the money, let's ask God." So John and Jennie told God what they needed and asked Him to give it. As usual, they did not tell anyone else about their need.

When they got to Detroit, some friends were waiting for them there, to say good-bye. One friend took John by the arm and walked with him across the station. He looked at John and said, "I don't know why, but all day long I have felt that I would like to give you this." Reaching into his pocket, he pulled out a $10 bill and put it into John's pocket.

John thanked the man, turned around and used the money to buy a ticket for his worker.

With the $3.50 that he had, John brought some food for his family to eat while they traveled on their next train to St. John's in New Brunswick, Canada. There they got on a boat to Liverpool, England.

GOD CARES ABOUT THE WASHING

Even though John had so little money, when he got off the boat he gave half of it to their waiter, as a tip to thank him for looking after them. In Liverpool all of their expenses were paid for by the transportation company, as the party waited there for a week.

By this time they had been traveling for a good few days and Jennie was keen to get some of their clothes washed. She spoke to John, because she knew that they did not have any money. John told her to send the clothes to the laundry and they would hope that God would give the money before they left.

John was so busy preparing everything else that he completely forgot about the clothes. On their final night in Liverpool, as they were going to bed, Jennie asked him about it. "I forgot," he said, "I'm so sorry."

"John, you are a typical man. Let me tell you what happened. I already knew that you did not have the money and I didn't have it either. So I decided to pray about it. After I had prayed, I felt that I should go to the laundry and find out exactly how much it was going to cost. I found it was £1.65."

"On my way back to the hotel, a man came up to me on the street, 'pardon me, but I feel I should give you this,' he said. And he gave me some coins. I went straight back to the laundry, counted at the money, and paid for the washing. The man had given me exactly £1.65!"

John and Jennie were so happy. This was one of those little things that helped them to know that God was with them.

Once more the whole group got on a train and travelled from Liverpool to London, where they were to get on their final boat and travel to Cape Town.

GOD WILL GET US IN

On the boat, John only had one English shilling left. The ship stopped at Madeira and John used his last bit of money to buy fruit for his children.

They would be landing in South Africa with not even a cent to their name.

John knew they had one more challenge ahead of them. Anyone who landed in South Africa had to show the immigration inspectors that they owned at least $125. If they did not have the money, they would be sent straight back home. He and Jennie prayed about this, until John had peace about it. It took over a week for them to get Cape Town, South Africa.

When the boat finally arrived the immigration inspector came on board and the passengers all lined up to show their money and be given a ticket that would let them get off the boat. Jennie did not know what they were going to do. John knew they were obeying God so God would take care of them.

"I'm going to get in the line with everyone else," he said to Jennie. "We have obeyed God so far. Now it is up to God. If they send us back, then there is nothing more we can do."

As John stood in the line, one of the other passengers touched John on the shoulder. He called him out of the line, over to the side of the ship to talk with him. John followed and they spoke for a few minutes. The man then gave him £42, worth $200.

John stepped back into the line, showed the money to the inspector, and was given the tickets so that they would be allowed into South Africa.

A GOOD ENOUGH HOUSE

Of course that was not the end of the challenges. Remember John and Jennie had seven children, not much money and no home to sleep in. There were nine of them and the children needed to be looked after. As with everything else on the journey they were simply trusting God to give them a home. After all, if God had called them to South Africa, God would give them what they needed.

That was how John and Jennie had chosen to live. They were faith missionaries; they did not have people back home who had agreed to give them money. Instead they depended on God.

The whole party got on a train to Johannesburg, where God had told them to go. Tom was the first off the train and a little woman came up to him. "Are you a group of American missionaries?" she asked.

"We are," Tom told her.

"How many of you are there."

"There are four of us."

"No," she said, "you're not the family I'm looking for. Do you happen to know if there is another family?"

"Well there is Mr. Lake here."

The lady looked at John, "How many are in your family?"

John replied, "There's me, my wife, and our seven children."

The woman cried out, "You are the family!"

John had no idea what the lady was talking about.

"God sent me here to meet you," the lady explained "and I want to give you a home."

John knew he could not afford a home that would be big enough for the whole family, so he told the lady that he would not be able to pay her. "We are faith missionaries and have no money to pay rent with."

"Don't worry about the rent," the lady said. "God wants you to have a home, so it's yours." The lady's name was Mrs. C.L. Goodenough. It sounds made up doesn't it, but that was her actual name. She had obeyed God and, through her obedience, had given the family what they needed.

That very afternoon John, Jennie and her family were living in a home complete with furniture.

God was clearly with them for the whole of their journey. But God had not called them to South Africa to bless them, He had called them there to see lives changed and souls saved.

CHAPTER 9

REVIVAL BEGINS

John Lake preaching

THE WHIRLWIND BEINGS

Days after John and Jennie had moved into their new home, a local pastor went on holiday and asked John to preach for him for a few weeks. John immediately agreed and so, on his very first Sunday in South Africa, he was preaching to a crowd of five hundred people.

Revival broke out. In those first few weeks, hundreds of people in Johannesburg came to know Jesus. Not only were they saved, they were also healed and baptized in the Holy Spirit. John was in the middle of a spiritual whirlwind, God was using him at a completely new level.

The presence of God was so strong in the meetings, and the people were so hungry for more of God, that the meetings often went on for most of the night. Sometimes they didn't stop until four o'clock the next morning. People all across the country heard about what God was doing and traveled to be a part of it.

During the daytime people would share what Jesus had done for them. With open Bibles they would show people that Jesus was not only real, but He could also save them from their sins. This was not just John's ministry, the whole church was learning to minister with the Holy Spirit.

John had to hire large buildings to fit everyone into the meetings. Then of course there were those who came to his house to ask John to pray for them so that God would heal them.

HEALING THE SICK

John worked nonstop. In the morning he would answer his letters and then he would open his office door. People would come into the office who wanted prayer for healing and John would spend a lot of time praying for the sick.

Jennie worked next to him as he prayed for the sick. She would welcome people into the house and even give them food to eat if they had to wait too long. Many of the people were very sick. Jennie did her best to make everyone feel comfortable.

Sometimes John would travel to preach elsewhere in South Africa. When he was away people still came to the home and Jennie would look after them until John got back.

On his return, John would go to his office and people would form a line to come in. Some of the people were healed instantly, others were partly healed, but some were not healed at all. John asked all those who were not healed to go into the room next door and wait.

John knew that Jennie had a very strong gift of discernment. God had given her the ability to work out what was going on and what the cause of a sickness was. She would go with John to all those who had not been healed. As she went to each one, God would often show her something that was stopping them from being healed.

To one she might say, "You have done this sin, but you have not said sorry to God for it."

To another, "You stole this item and God wants you to pay back the money to the person who you stole it from."

To another, "You need to accept that Jesus died to take away your sins."

God knew what was on the inside of each person's heart, and He showed Jennie things that she could not possibly have known if God had not spoken to her. Many would immediately confess their sins to God and repent, once they had been exposed by the Holy Spirit.

John and Jennie would pray again for them and they would be healed. Others refused to repent or to deal with the issues that God had shown. They left as sick as when they had come.

HELPING THE POOR

These were clearly supernatural times. John was driven, not by a hunger to see the supernatural, but by a love for God. Even though he and Jennie did not have much money, they would still feed anyone who came to their house. Jennie got used to making a meal stretch a bit further, when John would come home with several guests unexpectedly.

John often went to buy the groceries. When he did Jennie did not know what he was going to come home with.

One time Jennie asked John to go to the shops. John went and spent all their money on food for the week. On his way home he met a lady whose husband had died. She was a widow and she had hungry children to feed, but no food to feed them with.

Without even thinking John gave her all the food that he had just bought.

When he got home he had to explain to Jennie why he had no food. Jennie understood, because she was not only his wife, she was his partner in all that God had called them to do.

There were many people who needed help and many of them came to John for that help. He was so busy that he did not even get to see a great deal of his family. All this time Jennie knew that he loved her very much and that he loved his children. They never went hungry, God always provided for them.

EXHAUSTED BY LIFE

Life was very busy for the Lake family. Not only did they have seven children to look after, but it seemed like all of Africa wanted their help.

John got tired at times and would go away from home to have a rest. He never got to rest much. Once people found out where he was they would come from all over the place to ask him to pray for them. John loved people so much that he couldn't say no to them even though he needed to rest.

John left Jennie and the children behind and crowds of visitors would still come to the house. She didn't get to rest much. In fact Jennie didn't even have time to take a rest in the day, like other woman in South Africa did. She was so busy helping John, and when John was away she was busy helping others and her children.

Jennie looked after everybody except herself. John didn't notice that his wife was getting completely exhausted.

After over one year of ministry in South Africa, John had been preaching in the Kalahari Desert. God had used him there and he was now on his way home. On December 22nd, 1908 when he got back home he was hit with the worst news that he was ever to hear in the whole of his life.

Twelve hours earlier Jennie had died.

John was devastated. He had prayed for Jennie to be healed before and had seen her brought back from the very brink of death, but this time she had gone to Heaven and would not be coming back. Jennie was his best friend, his partner in ministry, the mother of his seven children, and his dear, dear wife. Now she had gone to be with Jesus.

John felt so much pain. Even though he still had the rest of his family, nothing was the same without Jennie.

The next year, in 1909, John decided to go back to America to get more support for the ministry and to bring more workers to help with the revival. It was hard for John to keep on going without Jennie, the sadness was so strong. Yet again it seemed like death and sickness had won, but he knew that God still had more work for him to do.

God supernaturally gave him $3000, so he and all the workers who had agreed to help him, were able to go back to South Africa, to carry on the work that God had begun. Jennie was now with God in Heaven, but God was still with John, as he stepped back into South Africa.

CHAPTER 10

A HEALING ANOINTING

John Lake

THE PLAGUE KILLER

As soon as John returned to South Africa, in January 1910, he found that there was a plague sweeping through the nation. One out of every four people had already died and the plague was still spreading. Nobody wanted to help the sick people, because they were afraid that they would end up catching it.

The government did not know what to do. They offered £1000 to anyone who would look after the sick. John and his workers all set straight to work, but they refused to take the money. They worked for free.

John went into homes where people had died and carried them out to be buried. John organized a whole army of people to dig the graves and more people to build the coffins. So many people had died that they couldn't even buy enough wood for the coffins. Some people were wrapped up in blankets and buried. They could not even spare the blankets for others, as they needed them to look after those who were still alive.

The doctors noticed that although John was touching the dead bodies, he did not wear a mask, or even a pair of gloves. They could not understand how he was not getting sick. More than that, they noticed that some of the sick people were healed when John prayed for them.

John told the doctors that the power of the life of Jesus was able to conquer all death and sickness. "God's life is flowing through me," he explained. The doctors thought he was talking nonsense so he asked them to do an experiment.

"Find somebody who has just died from the plague and take some of the fluid from their lungs. Examine it under the microscope and tell me what you see."

The doctors found masses of germs still living and moving around.

Then John shocked the audience. "Put these germs on to my hands and you will see the germs die." The doctor did what John told him to and all who witnessed it were amazed as they looked through the microscope and saw the germs die.

The life of Jesus, living in John by the Holy Spirit, was so strong that the plague could not survive on his hands.

SPIRITUAL WARFARE

God called one of John's friends to pray against the plague. He prayed for days on end, without getting a breakthrough. One day John walked past him and asked how he was getting on. "I'm nearly there," he said, "Will you help me pray through this last bit?"

John knelt down next to the man. The Holy Spirit then showed him a whole crowd of demons, like a flock of sheep. Both John and his friend rushed against the demons, sending them back to hell.

The next morning, when they woke up, the plague had stopped!

HEALING PAPERS

John saw healings happen, like in the New Testament days. He had a regular newsletter that he sent around. Before it was sent out, the church would lay hands on the papers and pray for the papers to be soaked in the power of the Holy Spirit so that when people would touch and read the papers they would be healed. Just like the handkerchiefs and clothing were filled with power by being in contact with the Apostle Paul, in Acts 19:12.

Many people were healed from sickness as they read the newsletters. The people of God were so full of God that they were changing anything that they came into contact with. God did miracles that restored parts of the body, miracles that healed parts of the body and even miracles that created body parts that were missing.

In one meeting a lady, called Mrs. Ulyate, stood up and came to the front of the church to ask for prayer. John asked, "What's the matter?" Mrs. Ulyate said nothing. So John asked Jesus to tell him why this lady was suffering. Instantly the Holy Spirit moved John's hand down to the lady's stomach. He prayed for her and she thanked him.

Later on John met her and discovered that she had been completely healed of stomach cancer.

He asked her, "Why didn't you tell me what was wrong?"

Mrs. Ulyate replied, "I was not sure if God was really with you or not. I thought that if God was with you, then He would tell you what was wrong with me. And He did."

Her son, who was twenty years old, was completely deaf in one ear. He'd had an operation where they removed the eardrum and some of the bones in the ear. When he was prayed for, God recreated the bones and the eardrum that had been removed, and he was immediately able to hear perfectly.

HEALING ROYALTY

Word of this move of God spread around the world and John began to get requests for prayer from all over the world. In the same way that he had called on John Dowie to help him pray for his family, now people were calling him, asking him to pray with them.

On one occasion he got a message from the Queen of Holland. She had been trying to have a baby. She had been pregnant six times. Each time the baby died before it was born. She asked John to pray that she would have a baby that would be born alive and healthy.

John prayed for her and sent back a message that her prayer had been answered. Less than a year later, the queen gave birth to her first child.

CHAPTER 11

A MAN OF CHARACTER

John Lake

LOVE YOUR ENEMIES

God didn't only use John Lake to heal sick people. Since John's baptism in the Holy Spirit he became more like Jesus, showing love to all people. He worked to the very point of exhaustion in South Africa, because he loved the people. If anyone asked him to come and pray for them, he would go.

He never turned away anyone who was sick, even if they came in the middle of the night.

John loved people very much, and did not hold grudges against those who wronged him. One Christian man had something against John. John had often spoken about what a great Christian this man was, how he loved God and was a real servant of the Lord. In spite of this the man had something against John.

He wrote a twenty-four page letter to John, to let him know about the issue. When John got it, he could have been angry. He could even have refused to speak to the man. Instead, John went to see him.

The man could not believe it; John had come to his home! He thought John would never want to speak to him again. Instead John went to make peace.

God had given John great authority in the Church. John did not use that authority to tear people down. Instead he wanted every Christian to understand that they were kings and queens before God. He did not want to be the superstar preacher, he wanted the whole Church to show Jesus to the world.

I'LL TELL YOU WHAT I REALLY THINK

Of course John was still human. He still had to fight with himself sometimes to do the right thing. One day someone had annoyed John so much, that he decided to write them a letter. He lay on his bed imagining the letter he would write. One of the things he wanted to write went something like this: "You great big cow, grow up, be a man and stop annoying me!"

John knew this was not what Jesus would want. After a little more thought he went to his secretary and dictated a letter. When she had written the letter, she gave it to him to sign.

As he read it through he realized that although it started off okay, there was still a nasty tone in the letter. He didn't sign the letter, instead he went upstairs to pray. Twenty minutes into his prayer time the phone rang. It was the same man on the phone. They agreed to meet and spent the next three hours together having a wonderful time.

John could have sent the rude letter, in fact part of him really wanted to send it because he was so annoyed. However, he decided to pray about it first until Jesus had worked in him and he was not annoyed anymore.

John was always thinking of other people. He would do anything he could to help others, even if it meant trouble for himself. He simply loved people. Some preachers around John's time would spend time preaching about how evil everyone else was. Their words were full of judgment. John's aim was to show people how great God was and to let them experience His forgiveness.

WORDS OF KNOWLEDGE

One day a woman came to see John, while he was resting. She begged him to pray for her. She was an alcoholic and wanted to be set free. As John looked at her, God showed him something. "Before I can pray for you, what about the £250 worth of jewelry that you stole from that home." God even gave John the address of the home.

The woman broke down in tears. Please don't hand me in to the police. "Please don't tell the people that I stole it." John told her that he would do nothing of the sort. After all it was God who had shown him. If it wasn't for that he wouldn't have known anything about it.

She repented and John prayed for her. From that day on she did not drink any more. Instead she spent her time working hard for the kingdom.

A few days later a woman came to John. It was her jewelry that had been stolen. She wanted to know if the other lady had told him all about it. John refused to tell her anything. Instead he ended up telling her how Jesus could forgive her sins. The lady broke down, wept and gave her heart to Jesus.

As she left, she asked John to let the other lady know that she was forgiven for stealing the jewelry and it would never be mentioned again! John loved it when people met with God.

COMPASSION ON A THIEF

One day he caught a young man trying to steal his car. He asked the man what he wanted the car for. The man explained that he wanted to take his girlfriend for a drive. John told the man that he was not planning on using his car until three o'clock in the afternoon, so if he wanted to, he could borrow his car until then. The man gave John his word and John gave him the keys.

Sure enough the young man returned the car on time.

Such a love for other people involves a sacrifice. John was no stranger to sacrifice and nor were his people. In fact John thought it was because of the huge sacrifice of the people that God kept on pouring out more of his Holy Spirit.

SACRIFICE

At one point in the ministry there were one hundred and twenty-five workers out across South Africa. Money got really tight, nobody sent money from overseas and there was very little money in John's pocket. At the end of each month he could not even send his workers $10. Then things got even worse and he could not even afford to send them $2.

John was responsible for the lives of these men and their families. As he could no longer afford to support them he called them all back home. Even to bring the men back home was a great sacrifice. He and his friends had to sell some of their clothes, some of their furniture and anything else that they could find to bring everyone together for a conference.

At the conference John shared with his workers how he could no longer support them. They asked him to leave the room, so that they could talk about this problem by themselves. When John came back he found that they had rearranged the chairs into a circle, with a table at one end. On it was some bread and wine ready for communion.

One man spoke up for the rest of the group:

"We have all decided that we want you to give us communion. We are going to carry on serving Jesus in the places that He has sent us to. We are going to carry on serving Jesus, even if we have to walk all the way. We are going to carry on serving Jesus, even if we end up starving. We are going to carry on serving Jesus, even if our wives die. We are going to carry on serving Jesus, even if our children die. We are going to carry on serving Jesus, even if it means that we will die. This work cannot stop, because there are too many people out there who still need to hear about Jesus."

The man continued, "You are no longer responsible for providing for our needs. We only want to ask you to do one thing for us: If we die, we want you to come and bury us."

Just like John had given up everything to follow Jesus, these men were willing to do the same. They knew it was very serious, but the call to preach the Gospel was even more important to them than their own lives.

In the twelve months that followed, John buried twelve of his best men and sixteen of their wives and children. They had lived with barely enough food to eat, if only they had had enough, they would have survived.

Jesus died on the Cross for us; He gave up His life for us. These men gave up their lives, willingly, so that others would hear about what Jesus had done. There was no greater sacrifice that they could have made.

MISSING FRIENDS

Right in the middle of all of the miracles and amazing things that God was doing, there was still great pain and a lot of sacrifice. Not only had John seen his workers die, he had also been persecuted by some people. Don't forget he had also lost his dear wife Jennie since he had moved to South Africa.

Then, in December 1910, only a year after Jennie's death, Tom felt it was time for him to move on. John and Tom had worked together for years. They had preached together regularly since the time when they had met in the city of Zion and they had been through many things together. Tom was John's best friend, and now John had to carry on without his support.

John was not alone. He still had his workers around him, and more importantly he still had the call of God to be there. The Holy Spirit was still with him, but he really missed his friend Tom. At times John wanted to give up, so God sent people to encourage him to keep going. Letters came in from many people thanking him for his ministry.

Jesus is more interested in our character than in how much of His power we can display. A strong character is needed most, when hard things happen to us. John was not just a man that God used; he was a man of great character. No matter what happened, or what he was feeling, John kept on serving God. God could trust John with His power because He knew that John had a strong character.

CHAPTER 12

GOD'S SUPERNATURAL POWER

Boy healed at the Spokane Healing Home

TOO POWERFUL TO TOUCH

God gave John so much authority in the spirit. In fact John spent a lot of time teaching Christians how much authority God can give them, if they walk close to Him and obey Him. John was so full of God's Spirit, while in South Africa, that there were times when people could not even come near to him. They would walk up to him to shake his hand, and would fall down on the floor under the power of God.

Once, when John was preaching in a meeting, a man kept standing up and interrupting John. This happened a few times and it was stopping people from hearing what God had to say. Finally, John pointed his finger at the man and told him to sit down.

The man dropped to the floor and lay there for two hours! God agreed with John and He made sure that the man did not interrupt again. Afterwards the man said it was like a bullet had gone straight through him and he could not get up.

Sometimes when John laid hands on people they fell to the floor so violently that John was worried they may hurt themselves. It was as if the power of God, that John was carrying, was too strong for them to cope with. He asked God about it and God told him to hold his hand a distance away from them. The people still fell over, but in a more gentle way. Also people couldn't say he was pushing them over, as he wasn't even touching them.

John didn't just pray for the sick and preach, he also cast out demons.

JESUS VS. DEMONS

A group of people called the Indian Yogi came to him one day. The group was made up of a range of different people. Some of them were priests of one religion; others were priests of another religion. Some of them were hypnotists, who were able to put people into trances. It was a very strange mix of people.

The one thing that joined them all together was their interest in supernatural things. They loved to have strange experiences and move in the spirit realm, though for many it was a very dangerous thing to do as they were using demonic powers.

They had heard of the amazing supernatural things that were taking place through John Lake and so they had decided to meet with him. They wanted to see this power at work. Perhaps they wanted to see if they could share that power, or perhaps they wanted to prove how great their own power was. Whatever the reason, John was ready to confront the evil forces at work behind them.

John agreed to do a demonstration with them, as long as it was done in public. John knew that God was more powerful than any power that they knew, and he didn't want them to be the only ones to see it. He wanted to make sure that everyone else would see it too. He invited them to choose a building that could hold lots of people. The best building they could think of was his church as it was one of the largest buildings around. Then John challenged them to see if they could heal the sick.

The Indian Yogi talked about it together and agreed to his challenge. They chose one person from the group to represent them. His name was Professor Henerson and he was a hypnotist. They also decided on which sick person they were going to try to heal.

Professor Henerson had been trying to heal a lady many times by hypnotizing her. One of her hips was locked in position so she could hardly move her leg. The professor hadn't managed to heal her yet, but he brought her out in front of everyone and tried again.

After a while John got bored of waiting for the professor to heal the woman. John knew that the man didn't know God and that he didn't know God's power. If John didn't step in the lady would never be healed.

John told the professor to stand back. Then he called some of the Christians to come and pray with him. John placed his hand on her and said simply, with authority, "In the name of the Lord Jesus Christ I command this hip to become unlocked." Instantly she was healed and could walk around.

John knew that Jesus had done it, but there was something else that he wanted to see happen. Something else that he would need God's help for. John waited on God, until in an instant the Spirit of God came on him. He felt God's authority rising up inside of him as he turned to Professor Henerson and spoke.

"Are you the man who has been hypnotising this lady for two years, taking her money from her? In the name of Jesus Christ you will never hypnotize anyone else." John grabbed the Professor by his coat and struck him on the shoulder, saying, "In the name of the Son of God come out of him." Immediately the hypnotic demon left the professor, and he never hypnotized anyone again. He had to find himself a proper job.

JESUS VS. VIOLENCE

One day John was called to pray for a man who had been drinking too much alcohol. Now that he had stopped he was suffering from something called delirium tremens, a condition that can cause shaking and hallucinations, so that the person looks crazy and out of control.

This man's grown up sons had tried to keep him safe. Even though there were four of them and they were all strong, their dad was too strong for them. In his craziness he had almost killed them all.

When John arrived at the house he found that the man had been locked up in a room. John asked for the key. The wife looked at him; she had seen her husband almost kill her sons. She did not want to see any more violence. She was scared of what was going to happen to John and refused to give him the key.

But John knew God's power. He knew that it says in 1 John 1:4: "He that is in me (God's Holy Spirit) is greater than he that is in the world (the demons)." After a bit of persuading he managed to get the key from the lady. John unlocked the door, walked into the room with the man and locked the door behind him. Then, John put the key into his pocket to keep it safe.

John looked around the room and saw the man, lying in one corner. It looked like he was asleep. John approached the man. As he got nearer the man crouched and growled at him. He looked and sounded like a lion preparing to pounce on its dinner.

John crept forward slowly, an inch at a time, repeating the words of 1 John 1:4 in his head. After around half an hour he was near enough to touch the man. He felt the Spirit of God working in him and grabbed hold of the man tightly.

He found himself looking straight into the man's eyes. There looking back at him he saw a demon inside the man. John cast the demon out in the name of Jesus and the man became still and calm. He had returned to his normal self.

God's power was at work in many different ways setting people free.

JESUS VS. INSANITY

One time John was in a church meeting, when one of his friends got up to speak, "I have been in this church for four years and seen God do incredible miracles. Today I feel so bad. God has shown me that I have not once asked for anyone to pray for a cousin of mine. She is in a mental hospital in Wales, completely out of her mind."

John was moved by his friend's request.

He invited the whole congregation to join him and pray for this lady. John knelt on the platform and started to pray. As he prayed he could feel the faith of the whole congregation. They were all praying and agreeing together in unity. John knew that God was going to do something.

As they carried on praying, John felt like he was being lifted up out of the building, over South Africa, passing over the seas to Wales. There in the middle of a little village he saw, in the spirit, a building that he knew was a mental hospital.

As John went into the hospital he found himself in a room with a lady. The lady had been tied to the bed, because she was so crazy that she was in danger of hurting herself and anyone else that came near her.

John put his hands on her head and cast the demon out of her in the name of Jesus. The lady's face became calm and she was no longer crazy.

All this time John had been kneeling on the platform in his church in Johannesburg, South Africa, yet it felt like God had taken him to Wales to cast out the demon.

Later a letter came from Wales. "A strange thing has happened. Last Sunday our cousin who was in the mental hospital was suddenly and instantly healed by God. She is completely well." The healing had taken place at the exact moment when John and his church had been praying together in South Africa.

LOVE AND SALVATION

Of course with God showing this much power, some could be distracted by it. God had prepared John for this danger. John's focus was not on the miracles, but on God and on the people God loved. Without love, all of these miracles would be pointless.

These smaller miracles all point to a much greater miracle, that God saves people not only from sickness but also from their sin. If everyone is healed, but nobody is saved, then the healings have no lasting meaning. Salvation from sin is the biggest need that every human being has. God wants us all to be His friends again.

God had told John that he would be in South Africa for five years and now his time was up. Looking back on five years of ministry, there were many miracles and many hardships, but the real fruit of John's ministry can be found in the souls that were saved.

After five years of ministry, there was a church with 100,000 new Christians in it, spread between 625 different congregations!

These people were all learning how God could work through them as easily as He worked through John. Many of them were working in the same authority that John had discovered in God. 1200 of them had been raised up as preachers, who could travel through the country and continue to share the Good News of Jesus. These preachers, who were all from South Africa, taught the Word wherever they went.

The healings and miracles showed people that God was there, this led many people to discover the greatest miracle of all: that God forgives our sins when we believe in Him.

The work John started in South Africa is still happening today. The Apostolic Faith Mission is now the largest Pentecostal denomination in South Africa. John's time in South Africa had been truly remarkable. Now God had more assignments for John back home in America.

CHAPTER 13

IT'S GOOD TO BE HOME

John Lake and his second wife: Florence

SHARING WITH FRIENDS

By the time John landed in America, he was totally exhausted. He had spent the last five years working almost nonstop. Wherever there was a need, John was there. Whenever people asked for help, John was quick to respond.

So many people had looked to John as their leader in South Africa. Now he was back in America he wanted to spend time with people, not as their leader, but as their friend. Although John preached in different places, what he really wanted to do was talk with other Christians and hear everything that God was doing.

John met up with his friends and they talked about Jesus for hours at a time. Just as earlier in his life, he had had a hunger for more of God, now John had a hunger for time with other Christians. For that first year he often stayed up all night talking with a friend. He would talk through the night for a week at a time.

John, the man on a mission for God, who had given out so much to other people in South Africa, now needed time with other people to help him rest, relax, and enjoy fellowship with other believers. John didn't think he was the only leader in God's Kingdom, he understood how important it was to spend time with other Christians.

In the past John had been able to talk and pray with Jennie. They shared everything together. When she died there was no one in South Africa who had been able to fill that space in his life. Now God was refreshing John, as he spent time with others, sharing their company.

A SECOND FAMILY

God knew how much Jennie meant to John. God knew that, like the first man, Adam, it was not good for John to be on his own. So in 1913 John met, and married, a lady named Florence Switzer. John and Florence loved each other and their marriage was very happy. They had five children together in addition to Jennie's seven children. John was the father of all twelve.

One day, in 1913, John was sitting in a large meeting in Chicago. Suddenly he received an urgent message. "Your son, Otto, is sick with typhoid fever. If you want to see him you must come at once."

Immediately John left the meeting and rushed to get on a train to Detroit, where his son was lying sick in hospital. As soon as he got to the hospital, he took his son to a private room and prayed for him. Within five minutes, Otto had been completely healed. John stayed with him for a few days to be sure that he kept getting stronger. By the time John left Otto, was up and walking around.

John travelled away again, to continue preaching the Gospel and ministering to people. But after a month, he was surprised to receive another message. This one told him that Otto was sick again, the typhoid fever had returned. Once more, John rushed to his son's side to pray.

This time he could feel the devil at work. He could hardly pray, but he was firm in his spirit. He was not going to let his son die. The devil could do his best to try and kill his son, but John knew his God. He spoke out a challenge to the devil, "Now, Mr. Devil, go to it. You kill him if you can." John knew that the devil would not be able to do it.

For the next five days and through the next five nights, John sat by Otto's bedside. Gradually his son started to get better. John had to hold on to God the whole time. After all his years of praying for the sick, John had found out that sometimes God heals instantly, like he had done with Otto the first time. Other times it can take much longer. At these times you have to hang on, and keep on praying.

Of course Jesus healed people instantly all the time when he was on Earth. John was not Jesus. Even after all his seeking for more of the Holy Spirit, he did not have as much of God as Jesus did. What John did have was the boldness to keep holding on. He trusted God. In the end Otto was healed completely.

As John traveled around America, he saw that there was a work to be done in the whole nation. The railway was the fastest way to travel back then, so John was delighted when he met up with one of his friends who ran the railway. His friend gave him tickets that would allow him to travel with his whole family on any of the trains. Once again John had been given what he needed to be able to do what God was telling him to do.

John used these tickets a lot in the years ahead. But God did not want him to travel too much yet. The first thing God wanted John to do was to set up a place where the sick could come and be prayed for.

CHAPTER 14

THE HEALING ROOMS

John Lake with mayor of Spokane, WA

WORD OF GOD'S POWER SPREADS

In September 1914, John felt it was time to settle down again for another five years. This time, he moved to Spokane, Washington and set up some healing rooms. The rooms were open every day and anyone who was sick could walk in and ask for prayer.

Many of those who came did not know Jesus. They had heard what God was doing and were desperate to be healed. Quite a number were suffering from sicknesses that the doctors could not cure. Every day one hundred people came to be prayed for, sometimes they prayed for as many as two hundred people in a single day.

With so many people being healed and coming to know Jesus, John had to start a church to help the people grow in their faith and get to know God. That was the beginning of the Apostolic Church. The church held meetings for six nights of the week and twice on a Sunday. Anyone was welcome to come and worship Jesus and be built up in their faith by the preaching.

During the daytime, John was busy. Not only did he work in the healing rooms, he also went into people's homes whenever they called him to pray for the sick. There weren't as many healings as in South Africa, and not everyone who came was healed, but God certainly did some amazing things.

TUMOR TROUBLES

One day a lady came in to the healing rooms. She looked pregnant. In fact, the doctors thought she was pregnant. Since then, over nine months had gone by and she had not had a baby. The doctors realized they had made a big mistake. There was no child within her, she actually had a huge tumor growing inside of her.

When John put his hand on her tummy, he knew at once that there was no child, just the tumor. When he told the lady, she lady broke down and cried. She was so upset by the news that it was difficult to pray for her that day.

The next day she came for prayer again and then went home. The following day she came back a third time. This time she did not look pregnant, she was back to her normal self with no bump. She could wear her ordinary clothes and was completely well. God had taken the tumor away, not even a trace of it remained.

I SAW JESUS

Another lady had six children to look after. When her husband decided to leave her, she did not know how she was going to cope because she was completely blind. She was so distressed. How could she take care of her children on her own when she could not see? She called her children around her and started to cry out to God in front of her house.

As they were praying, one of her children jumped up, "Oh, Mommy, there is a man coming up the path and he looks like Jesus! Mommy, there is blood on His hands and blood on His feet!"

Her children were frightened and ran off around the side of the house. Then the eldest child peered around the corner, "Mommy, Jesus is laying His hands on your eyes!" At that same moment she found she could see. Her children had actually watched Jesus healing her.

CHALLENGING THE NEWS REPORTS

In the healing rooms, legs grew back to their normal length, tumors disappeared, and people were healed from tuberculosis, blindness, deafness, paralysis and all kinds of diseases.

One boy's head was a really strange shape, it looked like his head was upside down and he could not speak. Doctors had said they would have to wait before they could operate on him, and even then they did not know if their operation would work. As they prayed for him the bones in his skull became soft and moved around. By the time they had finished praying, his head was a normal shape and he was able to speak.

The newspapers in Spokane published some of the stories, telling what God had done. These stories were read by many people in Spokane, who then came to the healing room to be prayed for. They were also read by members of the Better Business Bureau.

One of the jobs of the people in the Bureau was to check that stories written in the newspaper were actually true. So if someone claimed that their dog was able to fly, their cat could speak English fluently or their daughter had written a book when she was one month old, the men at the bureau would look into it to see if this really was true.

When they read all the claims in the newspaper of the amazing healings, they did not believe them. They knew they had to challenge John to prove the stories were true. John was more than happy to help them. He knew that God had healed many more people than the eighteen who had been reported in the paper.

First John called all eighteen people, whose stories had appeared in the paper, to come and tell the Bureau their stories. Then John gave the members of the Bureau names of many other people who had been healed throughout the city, so that they could be questioned as well. Finally John offered to pay for, and organize, a big meeting, where one hundred people would come and tell their stories of how God healed them.

He asked the Bureau to get a group of doctors, lawyers, judges and professors who could listen to all the stories and decide for themselves whether or not they were true. Remember John was a scientist; he loved things to be tested well. He also knew that all the stories were true. He knew what God had done, and was excited to have a chance to prove it.

They agreed to hold the meeting on Sunday, June 23rd, at three o'clock in the afternoon. In the meantime, the Bureau set to work interviewing people who claimed they had been healed, so they would be ready for the meeting.

Two days before the meeting was supposed to happen the Bureau sent John a letter. "We will not be coming to the meeting," they wrote. "We have seen and heard enough to satisfy us. These things did happen. Keep up the good work."

A couple of people in the Bureau came to see John privately. "John," they said, "we found out when we started asking these people questions, that you had not even told us half of what has been taking place here! It is absolutely amazing!" The proof they had seen was enough to satisfy the hardest of critics.

Even though the people from the Bureau were not going to come, John decided to hold the meeting anyway. He wanted everyone to know the amazing things that God had been doing. So that Sunday, as promised, one hundred people shared their amazing stories of how God had healed them.

THE MIRACLE BABY

One of them was a lady called Mrs. Graham. She was a nurse in the hospital and she had had an operation to take away some tumors from her womb. In the end they took out her whole womb. Without a womb, she knew that she would never be able to have a baby. Later on Mrs. Graham suffered from gallstones and had to have another operation. Unfortunately the operation did not go well, and she became very sick.

When the doctors could do no more for her, and it looked like she was going to die, she went to the healing rooms. She came in dying, but within minutes of being prayed for she was ready to leave in good health. Not only that, God also created a new womb inside her and the next year she gave birth to a baby!

God did many wonderful things in the healing rooms. Five years and 100,000 healings later, the government statistics showed that between the years of 1915-1920 Spokane was the healthiest city in America, thanks to God's work in the healing rooms. The mayor of Spokane even gave John a special award for all the good work he had done in the city.

After five years there, it was time for John to move on again.

CHAPTER 15

MORE TRAVELING—MORE HEALING

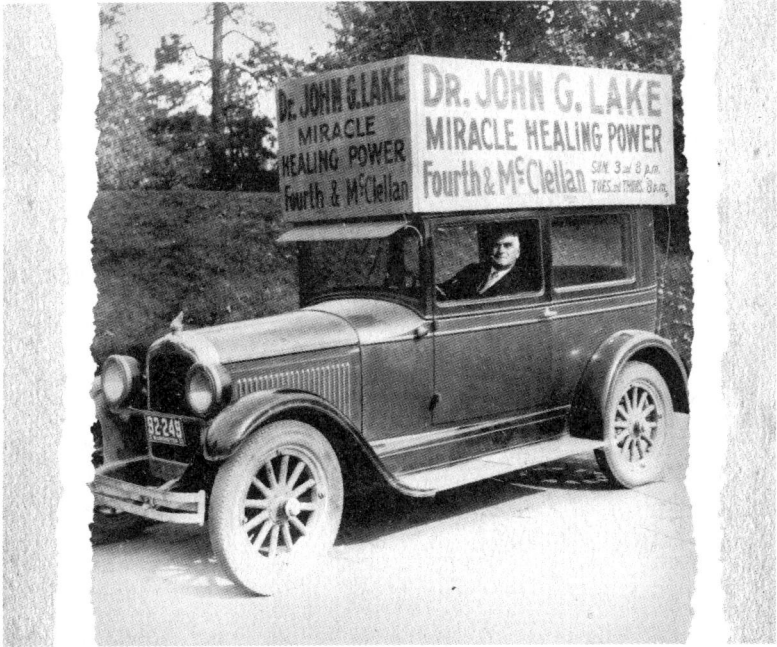

Mobilizing the message—John Lake on the road

BETWEEN LIFE AND DEATH

John and his family moved to Portland, Oregon where they started another church and set up more healing rooms. Once again, God worked to do amazing things and many people came to know Jesus.

One lady, Mrs. Stoughton, had such bad pneumonia that she was bleeding. John and his team knelt next to her bed and prayed for God's healing. As they were praying, instead of getting better, she stopped breathing altogether. Her heart stopped beating and for nine minutes there was no sign of life. John kept praying and miraculously signs of life returned, but she was still very weak.

Twenty more minutes passed, and she stopped breathing again, this time for eleven and a half minutes. Those around her bed could not give up without a fight. They carried on praying, and saw her revived, only for her to stop breathing for thirteen minutes. More prayer brought her back again.

Once more she stopped breathing and her heart stopped. Still the team did not give up. This time fifteen minutes went by, but there was no sign of life. The team held on to God. They would not give up and they knew God could heal her.

A full nineteen minutes later, at two-thirty in the morning, God's presence filled the room and she sat up in bed praising God, completely healed.

Her daughter, Beulah, had a cancer in the roof of her mouth. The doctors said they could remove the cancer but she would be unable to speak properly. The girl's heart valves were also leaking. She was healed from both conditions by God.

HAPPY DAY

Harley Day was eighteen years old when he discovered the healing rooms. He had never been able to speak. He hadn't even made gurgling noises when he was a baby. Harley also had a problem with his nose; he could not breathe properly through it. He had had six operations, but it was no better.

Some of his friends suggested that he go to John's church. When he went, John laid hands on Harley's throat and cast a dumb spirit out of him. Within a few minutes he was able to make noises, and over the weeks that followed his speech became more and more clear. It was like Jesus had prayed for him directly.

After more prayer, he was able to breathe through his nose. He chose to accept Jesus, not only as his healer, but also as his Savior.

After five years in Portland, John traveled a lot, setting up healing rooms in many different places.

GOD SPEAKS ITALIAN

One day John was in a railway station in Indiana, waiting for his train. While he sat waiting, he saw some Italian men on their way to work. John's brain started thinking. He walked up and down the platform as he thought, "I would love to talk to these men about Jesus and how He can save us from our sins. But they speak Italian, and I don't."

The Holy Spirit spoke to John, "You can speak to them."

John walked over to them and started to speak. As John began speaking a strange language came out of his mouth. John found that by the Holy Spirit, he could not only speak, but also understand Italian. He was able to tell them all about Jesus. Thanks to the Holy Spirit there was now no language barrier.

HANDY HANDKERCHIEFS

John knew God. In many ways he lived as if he was living in the time of the early church in the Book of Acts. He even saw people healed by handkerchiefs, like Paul had in Acts 11:12.

One day a lady was getting into her car. She was about to go for a drive with her son. Her son was driving. He didn't realize that she was not fully in the car, so he drove off. As he sped away she fell out of the car onto the ground. Her kneecap was broken and you could see the bone sticking out through the skin.

They called John, asking him to pray and send over a handkerchief. John sent a handkerchief that had been prayed over, which was placed on the lady's knee. Within fifteen minutes of it being put there, the bone had gone back in under the skin. Forty-five minutes later, she was up and walking around, as if nothing had never happened.

By 1924, John had started forty churches in America and Canada. John was one of the most well-known healing evangelists of his time.

John worked so hard, that by 1925 he needed to slow the pace of ministry a bit. For three years he worked at a slower pace and in that time God gave John a bigger vision of a modern day Pentecost, where every Christian would know the Holy Spirit and everyone would see God's power at work.

John was now ready for his final assignment from God.

CHAPTER 16

THE END

John Lake near the end of his life

"FOR YOUR GLORY, LORD"

In 1931, John returned to Spokane and set up more healing rooms. John had worked so hard for so long that his whole body was weak from tiredness. One day while he was there he started to lose his eyesight, until he was almost blind.

John was not so worried about himself, though he could hardly see, he was more concerned about what people would say if he was blind. God had used John to bring healing and the Gospel message to over one hundred thousand people in America alone. If he went blind now, he felt people might no longer believe in God, or that He could heal them and save them. People would mock God.

John loved to walk while he prayed, so he went for a walk to talk to God about it. He asked God to heal him so that God's glory would continue to shine in the nation. By the time John had finished his walk, he could see again clearly. He never had any more problems with his sight for the rest of his life.

He remained in Spokane until September of 1935. While he was there he built the church and worked in the new healing rooms.

One Sunday, John came home from a Sunday School picnic completely exhausted. Florence, his wife, encouraged him to stay home while she went to the church service that night. When she got home she discovered that John had suffered a stroke.

He could barely move and was unconscious for the next two weeks. Then, after two weeks of ill health, at the age of sixty-five, John G. Lake went to Heaven to be with Jesus on September 16th, 1935.

LESSONS FROM HIS LIFE

John's life was one that was always growing with Jesus. Like all of us, he made mistakes. John's biggest mistake and regret was probably the way he worked so hard and ignored the needs of his family while he was in South Africa. The main memory John's children have of him from that time is that he was not there. Even when he was around he focused all his time on his ministry, praying, helping others and so they did not see much of him. After Jennie died, John learned from his mistake and spent much more time with his children and his second wife, Florence.

John also learned early in his ministry that the focus of his ministry needed to be on Jesus, not on the amazing miracles that Jesus did, but on Jesus. Without Jesus there would be no miracles; with his focus on Jesus all things are possible.

John wore himself out serving other people. Perhaps he did it because of all of the sickness in his family when he was younger, or perhaps it was because God had given him a heart for people. Whatever the reason he always went to people when they asked him for help. He was never too busy or too tired for them, even if it was in the middle of the night. John would be there and stay there until his work was done. He loved people so much that he wanted them to know his God, no matter what the cost.

John didn't just show people the power of Jesus; he also showed the character of Jesus.

Of course John was still human, but he realized that God calls every believer to reign with Him. John was willing to give up everything and follow God. He gave up money, a good job, and even friends.

John also did not keep what he discovered about God to himself. He knew that he was not the only person who was able to follow God. He wanted everyone to follow Him at the same level.

John's life spent teaching other people about God was summed up well at his funeral by a man whom John had led to Jesus. He said, "Dr. Lake came to Spokane. He found us in sin. He found us in sickness. He found us in poverty of spirit. He found us in despair, but he revealed to us such a Christ as we had never dreamed of knowing this side of Heaven. We thought the victory was over there (in Heaven), but Dr. Lake showed us that victory was here (on Earth)."

When John was younger an elderly man had come into his office and prophesied that God would use him to bring revival to South Africa, and that God would use him across

America to stir up faith. Everything that the elderly man had said came true. The final part of the prophecy said that John Lake's life would be used to stir up faith in God in other generations.

If John's story has stirred up your faith, then why not spend more time talking to Jesus, praying each day and asking Him to reveal more of Himself to you. After all, if God can use John Lake, He can use you too if you are willing.

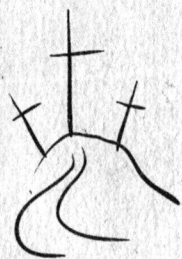

BIBLE STUDY FOR YOUNG GENERALS

Read Luke 9:21-25

1. What things do people try and get to make their lives as comfortable as possible in this world (even winning the whole world)?
2. By spending all our time and efforts in making our lives comfortable, how can we 'lose our lives', verse 24 (think about what God wants us to do)?
3. What things did John Lake give up as he followed God?
4. What do we gain when we follow God?
5. Is there anything that you would not want to give up for God? If there is, spend time talking to God about it.

6.

JOHN G. LAKE —ACTIVITY SECTION

REMEMBER THE BOOK

How much of the story can you remember? Test your memory by answering these questions.

Answers are given on page 126.

1. Which country was John born in?
2. Which missionary did John look up to as a child?
3. How did John Lake first make his money?
4. Why did John's wife, Jennie die?
5. How many people were saved while John was in South Africa?
6. Which city in America did John first open up healing rooms?

CHOOSE THE RIGHT ANSWER

Answers are given on page 126.

1. Who did John's healing ministry start with?
   A. His family
   B. A friend
   C. Someone who was not a Christian

2. After John was baptized in the Holy Spirit what was the first thing that changed?
   A. He saw more miracles
   B. He spoke to bigger crowds
   C. He saw things in his life that he had to change

3. How did John get the money he needed to go to South Africa?
   A. He earned it
   B. He asked people to give it to him
   C. He prayed and God sent it

4. How many churches did John plant in South Africa?
   A. 450
   B. 625
   C. 970

5. In what way did Spokane, Washington become the greatest city in America after John had ministered there.
   A. It was the largest city
   B. It was the richest city
   C. It was the healthiest city
6. How old was John Lake when he died?
   A. 65
   B. 75
   C. 85

1. A, 2. C, 3. C, 4. B, 5. C, 6. A.

Spokane in Washington.

4. She was exhausted from the work, 5. 100,000 people, 6.

1. Canada, 2. David Livingstone, 3. Running a newspaper,

ANSWERS

AROUND THE WORLD

John Lake lived in three main countries: Canada, America and South Africa. How long would it take to travel between these countries by airplane today? Time yourself to find out how quickly you can track John's journey from California to South Africa.

1. Monrovia, California, USA
2. Detroit, Michigan, USA
3. New Brunswick, Canada
4. Liverpool, United Kingdom
5. London, United Kingdom
6. Island of Madeira
7. Cape Town, South Africa

Write down your times here.

Date	Time Taken

PUZZLE IT

Decode this message using this code:

C→A D→B E→C

Yjcvgxgt aqw cum hqt kp rtcagt, dgnkgxg vjcv aqw jcxg tgegkxgf kv, cpf kv yknn dg aqwtu. Octm 11:24

— — — — — — —   — — —   — — —

— — —   — —   — — — — — —,

— — — — — —   — — — —   — — —

— — — —   — — — — — — —

— —,   — — —   — —   — — — —

— —   — — — — —.   — — — — 11:24

FIND IT OUT

John Lake was a man of Science. He like to ask questions and gather evidence. He was also a man of faith who believed the Bible is true. He encouraged Scientists to look at his faith and examine the evidence.

Use your scientific skills to examine creation up close.

YOU WILL NEED

- A magnifying glass or microscope

- Access to nature

WHAT TO DO

1. Look at nature close up:

    a. Choose some plants or insects and examine look at them with a magnifying glass.

    b. Take a close up photograph of an insect or plant and zoom in.

    c. Use a microscope and follow the instructions to look close up.

2. Draw diagrams or pictures of what you can see.

3. Use books or the internet to help you label the different parts of your diagram.

QUESTIONS TO THINK ABOUT

1. What do you learn about what you can see?

2. Can you learn anything about Creator God from what you see?

FOR FURTHER RESEARCH

1. Look at the structure of a plant/insect in a book and learn what each part does.

2. What do all created things have in common?

YOUR TURN

John Lake started a movement called the Apostolic Faith Mission in South Africa. This movement still exists today. Read about their work and see what they are doing. Write a report on their work. You may want to think about how John Lake's ministry still effects the church of today.

GET CREATIVE

Read the first part of chapter 10 again and do your own research on the plague in South Africa. What was the difference between the government workers and John Lake's workers who helped with the plague?

Create two posters: The first poster should be from the government of the time giving their workers advice on how to protect themselves from the plague and what they would be paid.

The second poster should be for John Lake's workers: Think about what they needed to know before they started, which Bible verses would encourage the workers, and how much money they would accept from the government for their work.

PHOTOS

John Lake in his later years

John Lake

John Lake with two of his sons

AUTHORS' NOTE TO READERS AND PARENTS

Like John Lake, I believe that God can cure people miraculously today. However, I do not believe that this is the only way that God will work. God gives wisdom and knowledge to us to help us fight disease. Medicine has advanced much since the time of John Lake. Medical care can actually be part of God's plan for bringing relief and healing to His people. However, medicine still does not hold all the answers. I am in favor of both competent medical treatment and the power of prayer. I would not encourage anyone to neglect either of these at their time of need.

BIBLIOGRAPHY

Roberts Liardon, *John G. Lake: The Complete Collection of His Life Teachings* (Tulsa, OK: Albury Publishing 1999)

Roberts Liardon, *God's Generals: Why They Succeeded and Why Some Failed* (Tulsa, OK: Whitaker House 1996)

Wilford Reidt, *John G. Lake: A Man Without Compromise* (Tulsa, OK: Harrison House 1989)

AUTHORS' CONTACT INFORMATION

ROBERTS LIARDON

Roberts Liardon Ministries, United States office:

P.O. Box 781888, Orlando, FL 32878

E-mail: Info1@robertsliardon.org

www.robertsliardon.org

United Kingdom/European office:

Roberts Liardon Ministries

22 Notting Hill Gate, Suite 125

London W11 3JE, UK

OLLY GOLDENBERG

BM Children Can, London WC1N 3XX, UK

info@childrencan.co.uk

www.childrencan.co.uk

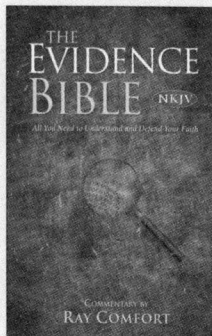

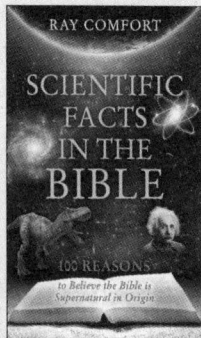

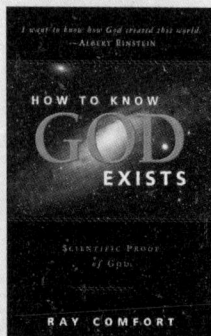

SCHOOL OF BIBLICAL EVANGELISM
Ray Comfort & Kirk Cameron

This comprehensive study offers 101 lessons on thought-provoking topics including basic Christian doctrines, cults and other religions, creation/evolution, and more. Learn how to share your faith simply, effectively, and biblically . . . the way Jesus did.

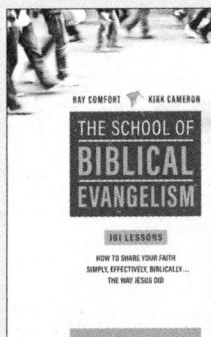

ISBN: 9780882709680

WAY OF THE MASTER STUDENT EDITION
Ray Comfort & Allen Atzbi

Youth today are being inundated with opposing messages, and desperately need to hear the truth of the gospel. How can you reach them? Sharing the good news is much easier than you think . . . by using some timeless principles.

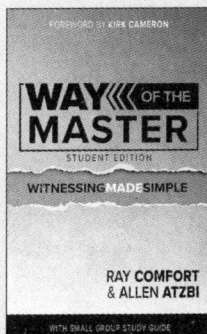

ISBN: 9781610364737

BRIDGE LOGOS

ALSO AVAILABLE FROM BRIDGE-LOGOS

BEAUTY FROM ASHES
Donna Sparks

In a transparent and powerful manner, the author reveals how the Lord took her from the ashes of a life devastated by failed relationships and destructive behavior to bring her into a beautiful and powerful relationship with Him. The author encourages others to allow the Lord to do the same for them.

Donna Sparks is an Assemblies of God evangelist who travels widely to speak at women's conferences and retreats. She lives in Tennessee.

www.story-of-grace.com

www.facebook.com/
donnasparksministries/

https://www.facebook.com/
AuthorDonnaSparks/

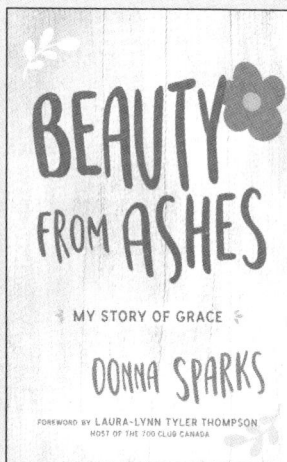

BEAUTY FROM ASHES

MY STORY OF GRACE

DONNA SPARKS

FOREWORD BY LAURA-LYNN TYLER THOMPSON
HOST OF THE 700 CLUB CANADA

ISBN: 978-1-61036-252-8

BRIDGE LOGOS

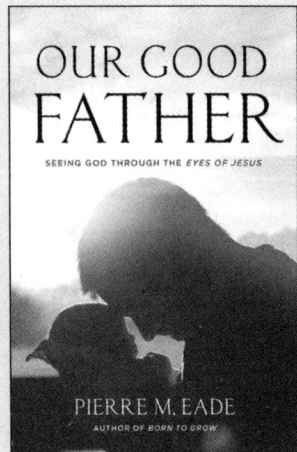